GHOST HUNTING
THE MOHAWK VALLEY

GHOST HUNTING
THE MOHAWK VALLEY

BY **LYNDA LEE MACKEN** WITH
CANO DAVY AND **MARCUS ZWIERECKI**

GHOST HUNTING THE MOHAWK VALLEY

Published by:
Black Cat Press
P. O. Box 1218
Forked River, NJ 08731
www.lyndaleemacken.com

Although the author and publisher make every effort to ensure the accuracy and completeness of information contained in this book, we assume no responsibility for errors, inaccuracies, omission or any inconsistency herein. Any slights of people, places or organizations are unintentional. For information, please contact Black Cat Press.

ISBN 978-0-9829580-1-8

Cover photo of Indian Castle Church courtesy of the Library of Congress.

Additional photo credits include Beardslee Castle page 81; Collinwood Inn B & B pages 39, 41, 48 and 55; Library of Congress pages 6, 23, 32 and 85; New York State Paranormal Research pages 11, 20, 35, 40, 70, 92, 97, 99, 104 and 105; Stone Mill of Little Falls pages 15 and 16; and Wikipedia pages xiii and 66. Illustrations courtesy of Clipart ETC: www.etc.usf.edu/clipart.

Printed in the United States of America by Sheridan Books, Inc. www.sheridan.com

Book Layout & Cover Design by Deb Tremper, Six Penny Graphics. www.sixpennygraphics.com

CONTENTS

* * *

* * *

Introduction

Mohawk Valley history is spirited with stories of the supernatural. Tales of hauntings enliven the rolling landscape where the blood of tenacious French and Indian War soldiers and loyal Revolutionary War patriots saturated the soil. Ingenious captains of commerce constructed stately homes and halls of hospitality where their restless souls still linger. Murderers slayed for taking lives hang on at their execution site. Although the eerie encounters arise from 18th century confrontations, 19th century trade and 20th century murder, the departed spirits who inhabit the region share a communal haunted history spanning centuries.

Manifestations of ghostly phenomena are extraordinary and mystifying. The Spiritualist Movement and organizations like London's Ghost Club and the Society for Psychical Research were founded in the 19th century to investigate paranormal occurrences. The present day pursuit of ghost hunting can be traced to these early societies. Over the last decade, popular television programs like *Most Haunted, Ghost Hunters, Ghost Adventures* and over two dozen other paranormal reality TV series in the United States as well as nearly 80 British supernatural broadcasts have spawned a phenomenal surge in ghost hunting groups.

Ghost Hunters premiered in 2003 on SyFy (previously the Sci Fi Channel). During the show Jason Hawes, Grant Wilson and their investigative team collect testimony from individuals about the alleged hauntings and research the history of the site being investigated. They also utilize psychic mediums or sensitive individuals with the ability to identify and make contact with spiritual entities. The program primarily focuses on the use of high-tech equipment to determine if a location is haunted.

While researching haunted places in the Mohawk Valley this writer unearthed compelling paranormal activity detected by numerous investigators from Central New York Ghost Hunters; IMOVES: Investigate, Manifestations, Orbs, Vortexes, Ecto, Spirits; Mohawk Valley Ghost Hunters; New York Shadow Chasers; New York State Paranormal Research; Northern New York Paranormal Research Society, The

Northern Paranormal Society, Rome Investigators of the Paranormal and Verona Paranormal Investigations. Above all, Cano Davy and Marcus Zwierecki, co-founders of New York State Paranormal Research (NYSPR), offered to enrich the stories by personally investigating the lion's share of the spirited sites.

GHOST HUNTER'S TOOL KIT

Among the various tools of the ghost hunting trade are digital thermometers and electromagnetic field (EMF) thermometers. (Abnormal cold spots in haunted places occur because spirits draw energy from the environment in order to manifest either visibly or audibly.)

Trifield®Meters which measure EMFs, night vision video cameras, audio recorders and laptop computers are also utilized. A popular gadget, as seen on *Ghost Hunters*, is the K2 meter. This handheld device detects changes in EMFs. Since spirits are energy beings, when an entity is present, the EMF is disrupted. The theory that ghosts can actually communicate with the living can be demonstrated by using the K2 meter as well. The operator prompts the spirits to answer questions by flashing the lights on the meter, twice for "yes" or once for "no," for instance. In most cases, the screen will flash with activity but only when asked questions!

Although experimental in nature, the Ovilus is another handy device which detects phonetic speech from the environment. The "Ghost Box," as it is sometimes called, works by measuring changes in the environment's energy field. According to the National Spiritualist Association, the Ovilus modulates the energy changes into audible speech using a synthesizer chip, an extensive dictionary of English words and a function that sounds out words. Amazing 21st century technology to ferret out ancient phantoms!

Modern day ghost hunting is all the rage but unfortunately age old skepticism, thanks in large part to unethical practices, casts a dubious shadow on anything unearthly.

"I shall not commit the fashionable stupidity of regarding everything I cannot explain as a fraud."
—C.G.Jung

GHOSTBUSTING SPIRITUALISTS

The fakery began in the State of New York near Rochester in 1848. Spiritualism emerged when Margaret and Kate Fox used "rappings" to convince their much older sister Leah, and others, that they communicated with the dead. The Fox sisters ultimately took their show on the road with Leah as manager. They reveled in their success as mediums for many years.

Forty years later, however, Margaret publicly confessed their performances were fraudulent and she demonstrated their method. The following year, Margaret attempted to recant her confession but the damage was done and their reputations ruined. In less than five years all three Fox sisters were dead; Margaret and Kate died in abject poverty. Still, Spiritualism flourished as the Fox sisters' admissions fell on deaf ears. Divulging their secret then retracting it provided both believers and skeptics with reason to support their cause, so the controversy continues.

American magician Harry Houdini opposed the Spiritualist movement in the 1920s following his mother's death. Houdini insisted Spiritualist mediums employed trickery and he aggressively exposed them as frauds. Sir Arthur Conan Doyle, most noted for his stories about the detective Sherlock Holmes, refused to accept Houdini's exposés. Doyle believed Houdini was a powerful spiritualist medium himself and performed his stunts utilizing paranormal abilities—a view Doyle expressed in his book *The Edge of the Unknown*.

Closer to home, Amsterdam, New York native Benjamin Paul Blood also delighted in debunking Spiritualists who visited the Mohawk Valley in the late 19th century, according to journalist Bob Cudmore.

Blood was born in 1832 to an affluent Amsterdam family. He convinced his friend, philosopher William James, to produce an apparition using nitrous oxide gas, an anesthetic used in 19th century dentistry. James astonished the crowd with his spooky demonstration and thereby exposed a wayfaring Spiritualist.

Dedicated afterlife researchers themselves, Blood and James affirmed mystical occurrences can be genuinely sourced in spirit as well as physical matter (the fraudulent side).

Today's ghost hunters strive to continue debunking supernatural claims but to the contrary their findings overwhelmingly validate spirit survival. In the following eerie encounters, the departed spirits who inhabit the region actively interact with the supernatural investigators. The Mohawk Valley's spirits are seeking attention from the living for varied reasons but mainly they manifest to communicate their phenomenal existence.

"A freight of ghosts from Death's dominions come."

—Philip Freneau

BOONVILLE

HULBERT HOUSE

In 1812, the post riders, who delivered the mail, lodged at the Hulbert House and rubbed elbows with celebrities such as Thomas E. Dewey, Ulysses S. Grant, Horace Greeley, Franklin D. Roosevelt and General Philip Sheridan.

In the mid-1800s Boonville prospered thanks to the development of the Black River Canal and Black River Railroad. The Hulbert House served as a central meeting place for the captains of industry who turned the wheels of commerce. Then, as now, the hotel hosted convivial celebrations and entertainment events. Today the Daskiewich Family welcomes guests, *and* ghosts—to their inn, continuing a tradition begun 200 years ago.

The spirits of the dead who roam the inn are such a part of life at Hulbert House that the hosts regard their resident wraiths by name. "Wayne" is a spectral soldier who appears dressed in Civil War garb. He stealthily strolls throughout the building and is not only seen but heard. At times, his heavy footsteps resound in the still of night. One patron who observed Wayne even held the men's room door open for him. The good-mannered customer stared in disbelief when the soldier turned on his heels and disappeared into the wall!

Astoundingly, Central New York Ghost Seekers captured photos of the elusive Wayne. These eerie photographs are viewable on the hotel's website: www.hulberthouse.com. Visitors to the website can also listen to electronic voice phenomena (EVP) audio clips captured by the paranormal investigative team.

"Lucy" is a little girl ghost who also meanders throughout the hostelry. Her apparition most often appears in the cellar. The long-haired miss shows up in a dress and we can only ponder as to why her presence lingers...

Another pair of ghosts includes a colonial couple who walk hand-in-hand in an upper floor hallway. Others signs of unearthly life at the lodge are unseen hands that reach out and touch some diners while certain visitors discern the sounds of children playing upstairs.

When New York State Paranormal Research (NYSPR) co-founders Cano Davy and Marcus Zwierecki investigated the historic inn they achieved the following significant results:

"At approximately 3:45 AM on the third floor of the Hulbert House hotel in Boonville we started an EVP session. We asked if there was anyone here with us and if so why they were afraid to show themselves. We captured a male voice responding, 'We don't fear anything.' His voice is very deep. We captured our second EVP on the third floor at 4:15 AM. We asked the question, 'Why are you here?' The response came from what we believe to be a woman saying 'to pray' or 'to play.' We heard this response during evidence review. We also discerned a commotion coming from a third floor room. As we went towards the noise and entered the room we both experienced vertigo. The Trifield®Meter fluctuated from 2–9 mill gauss. The dizziness stayed with us for only moments then suddenly stopped along with the Trifield®Meter dropping back down to zero. While taking photos on the first floor we captured a shadowy mass for which we cannot find a logical explanation."

(Listen to EVP audio clips on the New York State Paranormal Research website: http://nysparanormalresearch.com).

Considering all the souls who passed through the hotel's portals over the course of two centuries, it's no surprise a number decided to stay. Their continued presence proves Hulbert House's hospitality is truly out of this world!

DANUBE

INDIAN CASTLE CHURCH

Joseph Brant (1743 – 24 November 1807) was a Mohawk military and political chief who allied with Great Britain during and after the Revolutionary War. Perhaps the most renowned Native American of his generation, Brant met with many significant leaders, including George Washington and King George III, during his lifetime.

Sir William Johnson acted as New York's appointed agent to the Iroquois. This Anglo-Irish official of the British Empire commanded Iroquois and colonial militia forces during the French and Indian War and achieved victory at the Battle of Lake George in 1755. Knighted for his success, in 1759 Johnson conquered the French at Fort Niagara.

Johnson prospered as the Commissioner of Indian Affairs for the northern colonies and grew in wealth. In 1769, Joseph Brant donated the land and Sir William provided the funds to construct an Indian "castle," an enclosed village protected by wooden palisades.

The Indian Castle Church is the only surviving colonial building of the native peoples' castles in New York State. Owned by the Indian Castle Church Restoration and Preservation

Society, the elegant, centuries-old church rests on a knoll among pine trees and ancient tombstones. Located on Route 5 South in Danube, the tiny white church stands vigil over Mohawk Valley travelers. The relic is visible from the New York State Thruway whose construction obliterated many historic Indian sites.

Cano Davy and Marcus Zwierecki, the NYSPR team, investigated Indian Castle Church on two separate occasions:

"On our first investigation at the church we captured numerous EVPs. The voice recorder was left unattended as we investigated the cemetery behind the church. The first EVP was a female voice telling us to 'Get out.' The second EVP we captured in the church. A man is saying 'I want you here' followed by what sounds like squeaking from the floor boards. The third EVP is a musical note played on the piano captured while we sat in a pew near the podium. Our K2 meter sessions generated positive responses and throughout the process we felt an overwhelming sense of being watched. The graveyard on the property is actively spirited as well. While in the cemetery at 12:30 A.M. we shot four hundred and thirty photos; two photos contain some ectoplasm mists."

Mohawk Valley Ghost Hunters also explored the historic site. Every crew member felt touched by an unseen presence upon entering the spirited sanctuary. Invariably something or someone brushes against them—some long ago entity offering their hand to warmly welcome the spirit seekers. In addition to making physical contact, the ghost investigators captured white spheres with their infrared cameras. These light orbs are commonly thought to hold spirit energy. Amazingly, in some cases actual faces are discernible in the ethereal globes.

EAST BETHANY

ROLLING HILLS ASYLUM

Spine-chilling screams resound in the old Genesee County Home on Bethany Center Road. Although the building was abandoned in the 1970s, shadow people still lurk inside the storied structure. Stacey Jones, the Founder of Central New York Ghost hunters is convinced the souls of former residents linger at the Rolling Hills Asylum and *many* others agree. Jones has probed over 750 haunted sites and she emphatically states that Rolling Hills is *the* most haunted!

Originally the location of a 1790 tavern which catered to travelers, a portion of the ancient stagecoach stop still exists. In 1826, Genesee County officials regarded the brick roadhouse the perfect venue for a poorhouse as the establishment stood at the community's geographical center. The energy generated by the neglected poor, orphaned and mentally ill and their cruel caregivers, is imprinted on the place and has established a hot-bed of haunting activity.

During the 1950s, the location functioned as a nursing facility for about 20 years and then sat vacant until the 1990s when the locale became a shopper's mall for a while.

In 2009, Sharon and Jerry Coyle purchased the property where history records over 1,750 deaths (and scores of those buried on the property). Since the couple's ownership, the site has experienced a "spiritual" transformation into a ghost hunting mecca. The Coyles operate ghost tours, historical tours and special community events such as art festivals and car shows.

The Travel Channel's *Ghost Adventures* program featured the Rolling Hills Asylum on September 24, 2010. Lead investigator Zak Bagans and his team captured numerous EVP and the remarkable manifestation of a seven-foot-tall man named Roy. Roy resided at the asylum because he suffered from gigantism, a condition characterized by excessive growth and height. His unmistakable figure was caught on videotape and his distinctive image appears in many photographs taken at the site. The entire episode is available for viewing on YouTube.

NYSPR's Davy and Zwierecki say:

"As you approach the building you get the feeling you're not alone. The first investigation was the day after Roy's 100th birthday. We set up in a hall where Roy's apparition has been seen on numerous occasions. Cano began conducting an EVP session. The first question asked was, "How was your birthday, Roy?" A male voice was heard coming from the vacant room to the left. Another investigator also heard the voice. After analyzing the digital recording it sounds like the voice responded

to the question—his reply was, 'Hectic.' Later
on in the evening while the investigative
group relaxed in the lounge, Cano took a
walk to investigate on his own. He stopped
halfway down a long hallway and began to ask
questions. Suddenly all the hair on his body
stood up and he realized he was no longer alone.
Cano snapped a photo and captured two entities.
Later on, the team set up a video recorder
on the second floor and left it for the night...
Upon reviewing this tape, just moments after
Cano walked away, a white swirling mist is
seen dancing in front of the camera. The great
evidence and personal experiences lead NYSPR
to believe Rolling Hills does in fact live up to its
haunted reputation."

LITTLE FALLS

STONE MILL AT CANAL PLACE

Erected in 1839, the stone mill remains the oldest building in Little Falls' historic district. The mill produced wool uniform cloth during the Mexican-American and Civil Wars and uniforms worn during World War II were embroidered here. Like many other mills in Little Falls, water from the Mohawk River powered the machinery.

Located at 410 Canal Place, David Taylor and Richard Vogt purchased the mill building in 2005. The first floor is open to the public and offers shopping and services. The second floor houses local businesses and a 50-seat theater venue.

When this writer contacted David Taylor for information about the reported hauntings he provided the following extensive, eerie report:

"Shadow figures appear usually around 5 PM, almost as if they are checking on the security of the

building. Two children (3 and 4 years of age) at one of the shops on the first floor were always carrying on conversations when they were in the older stairwell going to the second floor to get their hair cut in the salon...when mom asked who they were talking to they replied, 'the fireman on the stairs.'

Spots of fog in the middle of the night in the ice cream shop were noticed by the owner. Heavy items in the ice cream shop being knocked off shelves. Voices are heard in the ice cream shop when nobody is there.

Cold spots on the second floor in a few of the suites lasting only seconds, any time of the *day…and catching of shadow people (definitely not floaters in the eyes!).*

Walking or running on the 4th floor could be heard during the night/early hours of the morning. This floor is locked and nobody is up there, not even electrical power. A regular heard someone pushing a broom in the middle of the night on the 4th floor.

During a wedding ceremony performed in the lobby of the inn last year, all equipment shut down and stopped recording…during this time two coffee makers went funky and didn't work.

Started up equipment and again stopped working halfway through the ceremony. As a side note, all cameras started working after they left the building en route to their reception dinner.

The inn, even though it is only two years old, has had quite a few incidents. One guest had a figure looking in the window at him in a particular room, and this is on the third floor on the riverside. Same guest in the same room a few months later had someone moving the doorknob to the bathroom when he got out of the shower.

A woman experienced the feeling of someone sitting on the foot of her bed briefly in the middle of the night.

When we had the antique store on the first floor a few years ago someone was talking to me at the counter in a wheelchair, and they kept looking over my shoulder at the vintage clothing booth, and asked me why there was a fireman standing there with an axe in his hand watching over us...I just said that was our resident fireman and he is guarding the building. She was psychic and knew nothing about anything that was happening in the building at that time.

Equipment malfunctions with the electronics in the theater during certain shows. Recently we had a show in the theater on the second floor, and a legally blind person who usually comes to all shows said she saw two spirits during this show walk up on stage and observe the production.

I will say, we have positive energy here, nothing bad, and the New York Pennsylvania Paranormal Society team never got so much activity in the night they were here than they have done on any investigations. They were quite impressed, and I was shocked at some of the findings they discovered. Best we could tell is that our fireman died in a fire as stated in the past by a medium, but not in the building, in a fire in Utica, NY, but he actually worked the majority of his life in this building, so perhaps that spirit is here where he spent most of his life and happiness? We are still researching that one.

Oh, another interesting fact. My partner, Richard, would walk along the canal at times when we had no guests in the inn, and noticed lights on at the inn in a few rooms. When he got back from that side of the river to check on the rooms, there were no lights on. These were fluorescent lights in the bathrooms…that was a strange happening, as nobody was on the third floor.

Also, this early spring/late winter, when I fired up the granite fountain by the front door, when it was still cold and there were no bugs in the air yet, the exterior security cameras picked up many orbs, sort of heading towards the fountain and then disappearing up the face of the building."

When New York State Paranormal Researchers investigated the Stone Mill:

"We started by setting up our security system and digital recorders in the four most active rooms on the third floor. We then set a handheld infrared camera and recorder in the attic, basement and second floor hallway. Marcus and John began their night covering the attic and third floor while Justin and Cano focused on the basement and second floor. While down in the basement we were conducting an EVP session when Cano was suddenly hit with a cold breeze shooting through his entire body…more than just a breeze—the hair on Cano's right arm actually moved as if standing in front of a fan.

Cano Davy gets ready to search for spirits at the Stone Mill.

We looked for a reasonable explanation for this but were unable to find any open windows or openings to the outside that would cause this. Cano has been investigating for several years and this is the first time this ever happened. Also while in the basement Cano asked the spirits if they had to stay hidden to which they responded, 'Yes.' We then left the basement and headed up to the second floor. We left a stationary recorder in the basement and believe we captured a child's voice. We cannot understand what is being said but the voice is there. Marcus and John were in the attic using a device called the Ovilus. The Ovilus is equipped with a 2,000 word data base and enables spirit communication. While they were using this tool Marcus says, 'Can you say the word 'child," an immediate response is displayed—the word 'child!' We also captured a male voice in the Melrose Room, 'Getting tired.' This sounds like an older gentleman's voice. After covering our designated areas we took a break to discuss where each team would survey next. In reviewing the evidence, during this brief meeting a loud bang can be heard on the recorder placed in the attic. After we resumed, Justin and Cano headed to the attic. While conducting an EVP session we suddenly heard noise coming from the eastern point of the attic. We investigated the sounds but could not find a source. We heard about this claim... footsteps in the attic and unaccountable noises. This was a very interesting investigation for the team and we'd love to come back at a later date..."

HERKIMER

HERKIMER COUNTY JAIL

The Herkimer County Jail rose to prominence in 1906 when headlines broadcasted Grace Brown's infamous murder at the hands of Chester Gillette. The 1834 lockup housed Gillette during his spectacular front-page trial that resulted in his conviction and ultimate execution in the electric chair one year later. Theodore Dreiser's subsequent novel, *An American Tragedy*, was based on the crime and further enhanced the building's lore.

Attorney George W. Ward successfully prosecuted the notorious murderer. Ward's five-story home in Dolgeville, New York is presently operated as Ward's Pond Bed & Breakfast and allegedly is also haunted. Some say Grace Brown's spirit lingers at her family's South Otselic, New York farm house as well. This writer observed Grace's ghost hovering over Big Moose Lake where she was drowned by Gillette (see the author's *Adirondack Ghosts*). *Four haunted venues connected to one murder—amazing!*

Most believe the 19th century executions at the Herkimer Jail cause the haunting at the site. On February 28, 1887, Roxalana Druse from the Town of Warren hanged in the jail yard. According to Bernard Peplinski, a Friend of Historic Herkimer County, Druse murdered her husband, dismembered his body with an ax and incinerated his remains in a wood stove.

Hanging from the gallows snuffed out many criminals in Herkimer County. The location's haunted reputation rests on the sight of filmy apparitions hanging by the thickest of threads in back of the building.

One Ghost Seeker of Central New York was shoved into one of the cells. In reviewing the pictures taken during the group's inspection a spirit manifests near Gillette's cell and a giant light orb, thought to be spirit energy, appeared outside the jailhouse.

New York State Paranormal Researchers achieved astounding results during their survey of the property:

"This was a strange investigation because the only available time to research was from 12 – 5 PM so we had no choice but to take it. We did our normal routine of setting up in the most active locations that we were told about. Six infrared cameras, three digital cams and eight digital recorders were used along with the Ovilus and EMF and temperature readers. One of the main points of interest was Chester's cell. We began the investigation in this area of the jail. We just began using the Ovilus device a month or so ago so we are still getting

used to the way it works. We found out on this investigation the Ovilus would randomly say words but to our surprise a lot of what it was saying directly linked to either the Chester case or the jail. During our Chester cell part of the investigation the Ovilus said six words that we found very interesting. Marcus says 'Are you here with us?' The Ovilus says 'Yes I am.' Just randomly the device says, 'informant' which is something you are very likely to hear in a jail setting. The next word that it says that we found of interest was 'murder.' Now this could either be associated with Chester or just again a word that you may hear in a jail house. Marcus asks about Grace and the Ovilus says 'lake' which directly is linked to the Grace case. Then John asks about the Adirondacks, the machine yells out 'happiness.' (Grace considered her trip with Chester to the Adirondack Mountains as a kind of honeymoon). The last word we found to be the most interesting is the word 'trimester' which as you know is another direct link to Grace Brown as she was pregnant at the time of her death. Later on in the investigation while John was alone down in the basement he contacted a spirit through the K2 meter. All the K2 LEDs would light up then back down depending on the question he was asking. Marcus also tried this method of communication with the TriField®Meter and began to have the same results; we captured this on film. At one point Cano was using the ITC (Instrumental Transcommunication Box is simply an AM/FM radio that continuously scans up and down the dial without stopping, also known as a 'spirit box') Box and asked if they had ever heard of Grace Brown, to which a response of 'Grace' can be heard. All in all a very worthwhile investigation. One of the most amazing pieces of the night was when the Ovilus says the word 'sentence,' so I ask 'What was your sentence? How long were you here?' to which it responds 'years.'"

JOHNSTOWN

KNOX MANSION

The Knox Mansion is a historical house built in 1889 by gelatin magnate Charles Knox. Knox produced the world's first pre-granulated gelatin in the late 19th century. The revolutionary product significantly impacted modern cooking. Today the brand is owned by Kraft Foods but for several decades the gelatin product was produced in Johnstown.

Charles' wife, Rose, wrote recipe booklets to promote the gelatin's versatile use in molded desserts, salads and cold soups. Over a million were distributed every year. Knox allotted his wife a weekly stipend and permitted Rose to do anything with the money as she pleased.

When her husband passed away in 1908, Rose took over the business. Her first action was shutting down the factory's rear entry, formerly used by the women—all employees now entered by the front door, not only the men. Rose believed in sexual equality. When she overheard a top executive say he would not work for a woman, Rose asked for his resignation.

The progressive woman went on to establish a five day work week and two weeks paid vacation, an unprecedented benefit. Remarkably, under Mrs. Knox's leadership, the gelatin company survived the Great Depression without having to release any workers.

Many feel Rose's pioneering spirit still pervades her earthly abode. The Knox mansion is a national historic landmark and is currently owned by Marty Quinn who used to run the house as a bed and breakfast inn. The mansion boasts 42 rooms, an elevator, a grand staircase and a solid lava ash fireplace imported from an Italian castle. The residence retains mysterious cubicles as well. In the billiard room a small panel is secreted in a bookcase—most likely used for concealing valuables. A tiny, three-foot high portal leads to a hideaway off an attic bedroom.

Throughout Quinn's long tenancy, eerie anomalies occurred in the house. Inexplicably, lights and the television turn on and off. Curiously, fragile items are found broken and eerie footsteps resound. The owner said blankets are pulled off the bed during the night. Is Rose Knox the culprit creating these anomalies? She may be a frustrated spirit seeking to make her presence known.

Even Quinn's two daughters experienced unexplainable phenomena—Sara felt a presence walk right through her and Amy heard voices and sensed being watched. Overnight guests shared dozens of supernatural stories experienced during their stay. They claim to hear disembodied voices, endured cold spots and sighted specters including a phantom pianist. Some felt physically touched by an unseen presence. One visitor observed a male apparition carrying what looked like a doctor's satchel. This entity may be a previous owner's spirit—he was a physician who allegedly committed suicide. Furthermore, spectral children are heard in the mansion on occasion when none are present. A lot of people say they've seen a little girl's apparition.

A few detect a ghostly figure in the basement; believed to be the former landscaper. Kids, in particular, perceive the long-gone gardener who in life especially delighted in children's' company.

Adding to the creep factor is Charles and Rose Knox considered the number 13 auspicious and even designed their home with their lucky number in mind. For instance, there are thirteen tiles in the fireplace and thirteen steps on the grand staircase.

When ISIS Paranormal Investigators surveyed the property their digital camera stopped working and shut off by itself while photographing the Gold Room. Other unexplained anomalies occurred throughout the house with other cameras. When notes were compared among the team members they realized most of them suffered difficult breathing and vertigo. These symptoms are common at spirited sites and may serve as a barometer in determining if a place is haunted. Another researcher felt something grab his leg while in the Billiard Room and on the third floor, a fellow ghost seeker reported a similar sensation from an unseen entity.

On Halloween nights Quinn covers the house with cobwebs, scary paintings and sinister statues. He conducts a haunted house tour complete with costumed actors. Over 1,200 people show up to explore the decked out manse and enjoy some good old-fashioned scares. So, if you spot a ghost in a Knox Mansion window on October 31st it may not be a decoration...

LITTLE FALLS

FORT HERKIMER CHURCH

The Mohawk Valley's Old Fort Herkimer Church served as a refuge during the Revolutionary War when vicious rampages sent colonists into retreat at fortified settlements. During their first major onslaught in the region, the British incinerated every barn, house and mill. Patriots, protected behind the garrison's walls, watched in horror as flames devoured their homes with all their earthly possessions and their precious livestock driven off by the Redcoats. The intense emotional energy discharged during the ambush is imprinted in the 1756 Dutch Reformed Church where paranormal researchers detect otherworldly presences.

Originally painted to resemble stone, the edifice hosted a visit by General George Washington in 1783. Located on Route 5 South, the churchyard holds the earthly remains of Native

31

Americans, early settlers and those who bravely defended the country to preserve freedom.

Ghost hunters from IMOVES, (Investigate, Manifestations, Orbs, Vortexes, Ecto, Spirits), videotaped floating images on the church's tower and unexplainable hovering lights and orbs in the cemetery. One photo revealed an eerie, disembodied mustachioed face in the church window which can be viewed on their website: www.imoves.net. Below this casement is a headstone bearing the inscription: "John Ring, Esquire from Ireland who departed this life at the age of 30." Could it be John Ring whose countenance appears in the church window?

A popular theory among ghost investigators is spirits draw energy from any available power source in order to manifest. That's why batteries go dead and electronic equipment malfunctions. Such is the case at Herkimer Church. Thermal indicators, a ghost hunting tool, registered extreme temperature fluctuations by as much as 30 degrees. Cold spots, commonly experienced at haunted places, are an anomaly also attributed to spirits pulling energy from the environment.

MORRISVILLE

MORRISVILLE LIBRARY

Morrisville Public Library is a historic building located in Madison County. Civil War Captain Lyman Kingman built the picturesque, Gothic Revival cottage in 1855. Subsequent owner Susanna Phelps Gage donated her family home to the village when her parents Henry and Mary Phelps passed away. The library opened with 760 volumes on its shelves in 1903.

At times, Library Manager, Michelle Forward says she feels a presence while in her office. Undoubtedly, the most unexplainable event occurred on the second story when a chair lifted on its own and forcefully flew five feet across the room!

Ms. Forward said when the portrait of Susanna Phelps Gage was removed from the library for reframing the spirits took exception to its temporary absence. Books flew off shelves during the night and were found the next morning on the floor. In one instance as the librarian made her rounds reshelving books from a rolling cart she decided to call it quits for the evening. She parked the cart in a room and left. When Ms. Forward returned the next day, four of the books that were on the cart where she left it, were found on the hallway floor two rooms away. Perhaps the culprit is the disembodied soul whose footsteps are heard or maybe it's the incorporeal children who are often perceived laughing in the book depository...

NYSPR reports:

"We began our investigation at the Morrisville Library by setting up two teams—Marcus and Cano and Justin and John. Although the night was quiet, as the evening progressed it seemed as if whoever was there tried to avoid us. We did not capture any audio evidence at all but we did capture a few video clips from the K2 meter in response to questions. At one point we sat in an employee's office and began to read a scrap book about the library's history along with personal details regarding the property's original owner. Before we began reading we placed the K2 meter in the doorway and basically forgot about it. Twenty minutes later we were still reading the book when Cano glanced over at the meter and it was pegged all the way up... it was lit up like a Christmas tree! As soon as Cano noticed it and brought it to the other members' attention it stopped. It was as if somebody stood there listening to us read and when we became aware of his/her presence left. Another thing to note is the K2 meter is very sensitive to cell phones so we turn them off and leave them at base camp while investigating. We then left

the office and made our way to the library and started another K2 session. No responses except when Cano asked, 'Do you want us to leave?' to which the K2 lit up as far as it could. It was very interesting. Throughout the night we felt as if we were not alone yet felt the resident spirits were giving us the cold-shoulder (no pun intended!). Maybe they did not enjoy the intrusion or needed more time to warm up to us."

ONEIDA

COLLINWOOD INN

Owners Gerri and Brian Gray tout their Collinwood Inn as the world's first and only *Dark Shadows* themed bed and breakfast inn. *Dark Shadows* ran as a weekday gothic soap opera that aired on ABC television from June 27, 1966 to April 2, 1971. Unique in daytime television, ghosts were introduced about six months into the show's programming. The unprecedented series grew in popularity when vampire Barnabas Collins, as portrayed by Jonathan Frid, debuted as a character in 1967.

The Collinwood Inn is a 19th century Italianate Victorian mansion offering the visitor a choice of four guest bedrooms—all are named after a *Dark Shadows* character. Overall, the inn's atmospheric interior is achieved by antique furnishings and *Dark Shadows* memorabilia. Upon request, the hosts offer guests private showings of *Dark Shadows* movies and Victorian-style séances.

The New York State Paranormal Research investigative team reported:

"John Pauba and Justin D. Reynolds began their night investigating the basement area. The pair conducted an EVP session along with taking baseline EMF and temperature readings. As they made their way from the main room to the hallway, a faint voice can be heard saying, 'It's cold down here.' Their exit from the room was captured on a static night vision camera and after closely examining the footage neither John nor Justin are saying a word.

Marcus Zwierecki prepares to hunt for
ghosts at the Collinwood Inn.

*Digital recorders were placed in the attic,
the basement and in the Barnabas Room and
left unattended all night. While in the attic
conducting our investigation, the recorder in the
Barnabas Room captured what we believe to be
two audio anomalies. The first being a screech or
moan maybe from the phantom cat. Cano tried
to find a natural cause for this noise and listened
close to see if this sound showed up again some
other place on the recorders but it did not.*

Again in the Barnabas Room a male voice was captured saying 'Get out!' Cano tried to find a natural explanation for this but was unable. This voice is NOT one of the group members.

Cano and Marcus started their investigation in the attic. The first incident happened shortly after we began our session. Cano turned on the ITC Box and Gerri (Gray) held her voice box in hand when Cano asked 'Is your name Fred? Fred, are you here with us?' To which a response can be heard coming from the ITC Box

saying, 'Yes...I am.' Then moments later a voice is heard coming from Gerri's box saying. 'Did you hear that?' Next Gerri says, 'Come to me and say something please.' We hear two separate voices first a male speaking an obscenity then right after a woman repeats the same X-rated expletive. Last but not least we are walking down the attic steps and a loud whisper was captured on the recorder left in the attic saying, 'Come back.' The voice sounds like a man."

THE HOUSE OF MANY SHADOWS

THE HISTORY AND HAUNTINGS OF THE FARNAM MANSION

by

Gerri Rachel Gray

On the corner of Main and Stone Streets in the quaint historic district of Oneida, New York, stands a red brick Victorian mansion constructed in the Italianate style—a popular and highly fashionable style of architecture in 19th century America. The mansion, which is currently used as The Collinwood Inn Bed and Breakfast, was built sometime between 1862 and 1864 for a gentleman by the name of Stephen H. Farnam. It reflected his wealth and good taste with three fireplaces of imported Italian marble, ornate plaster ceiling medallions in almost every room, a grand staircase, tall paneled doors of oak, exquisite crystal chandeliers, eleven-feet high ceilings enhanced by thick and decorative plaster crown moldings and two matching sets of paneled pocket doors. During the late 19th and early 20th centuries, many lavish dinner parties, charity fundraisers and club meetings were held at the mansion and attended by members of high society.

Mr. Farnam (whose obituary described him as a well-known and highly esteemed citizen of Oneida) was born in Little Falls, New York, where he made his living as a blacksmith before becoming the proprietor of the Little Falls Axe Company. After relocating to Oneida with his wife Elizabeth and their children, he went on to become the successful owner of a hardware store, president of the National State Bank and president of the Glenwood Cemetery Association. Stephen H. Farnam was also one of the organizers and first directors of the Oneida Gas Light Company and served on its board of directors until his death.

Elizabeth Farnam, who passed away on February 17, 1885, was the first person to die in the mansion. Seven years later on the thirteenth of April, son Frederick James Farnam died in his bedroom after succumbing to consumption (as tuberculosis was commonly called in those days). On November 17th in the year 1897, death again visited the Farnam Mansion, this time claiming Stephen H. Farnam, who died from apoplexy. The funeral took place from his home and his body was interred in the Glenwood Cemetery.

Over the years the mansion has been home to a number of people from many different walks of life. In the early 1900s a locally famous woman by the name of Mary Dyer Jackson purchased it. An early activist in the women's suffrage movement, she was the first woman to circulate a petition in Central New York for the women's suffrage cause. She also founded the Progress Club in 1889 and became a charter member of the Madison County Historical Society in 1898.

The next owner of the house was Dr. Robert L. Crockett who specialized in ailments of the eyes, ears, nose and throat. Dr. Crockett was Mayor of Oneida from 1916–1917 before leaving to serve in World War I. An amateur botanist, the good doctor had a laboratory in the basement of the mansion, and he suffered a fatal heart attack in the lab on May 27, 1946. His widow sold the mansion to Dr. Chancellor Whiting in 1952, who in turn sold it to another doctor ten years later.

The last doctor to own the mansion, (whom we

will call Dr. H.), died in his bedroom on September 3, 1984. The cause of his death was colon cancer. His death came almost two years after the death of his wife. Her lifeless body was found in one of the small parlors on the mansion's first floor, which is currently used as a master bedroom.

The house was then purchased in 1986 by a couple who converted it into a bed and breakfast they called The Polly-Anna. They added four bathrooms and two private rooms with a Jacuzzi tub to the upstairs guest rooms and made some other changes to the house as well. They operated the B and B for a number of years until health issues eventually forced them to retire from innkeeping and put the house up for sale.

Ownership of the Farnam Mansion changed hands one more time before I purchased it in 2010 and began restoring and redecorating the house with my husband Brian with the intention to reopen it as a bed and breakfast. However, we didn't want it to be just another boring old Victorian B and B. We wanted our inn to be different with a unique theme that had never been done before. After considering a few different themes, we finally decided to go with one that would be a tribute to a television show we both loved as youngsters—*Dark Shadows*. We decorated the house with various *Dark Shadows* memorabilia, antique pieces from auction houses and my former antique shop and other items that resembled the props used on the show. We then christened it, The Collinwood Inn Bed and Breakfast.

A year or so before we made the Italianate Victorian mansion at the corner of Main and Stone Streets our new home, the house was featured in an *Oneida Dispatch* special edition article about haunted Victorian mansions in the area. I also talked to the lady who ran the Polly-Anna and she informed me that many years ago someone who had visited her at the house witnessed the ghostly apparition of a man reflected in a mirror in the parlor and wearing what appeared to be a uniform dating to the Civil War era. She also told me that on several occasions she heard music and the sounds of people talking and laughing coming from the parlor when no one was in there... at least no one of this world. She described the spirits to me as "happy" and said neither she nor her husband ever felt afraid or threatened during the entire time they lived here.

My husband and I also had an interesting chat about ghosts and spiritualism with the man who sold us the house. I must admit we were a bit surprised when he came right out and admitted

to us that he believed the house was haunted and we were fascinated and eager to hear all about the spirits that he and his wife had encountered in the old Farnam Mansion. One was a full-body apparition of a man that appeared in the main hall near a large antique mirror and whom he later identified as being Dr. H. (We later learned that this particular mirror, which we initially thought was original to the house, was actually a piece owned by Dr. H. and brought with him when he moved here from the New York City area). He also said his wife claimed to have seen the full-body apparition of a woman wearing a Victorian style dress gracefully descending the grand staircase and then vanishing like mist before her very eyes. Rather than being terrified (as I'm sure would be the natural reaction of a good many home-buyers) we were actually rather intrigued by all of this and felt we were in for what could only be described as an out-of-the-ordinary adventure.

Not long after moving into the mansion, on the anniversary date of Dr. Crockett's death, Brian and I went downstairs into the basement and attempted to make contact with the spirit of the doctor. With only the flickering flame of a candle to light our way, we walked around in the empty cobwebbed rooms of the basement, speaking out loud to the doctor and reassuring him (and any other spirit or spirits that might have been within earshot) that we meant no harm and only wished to introduce ourselves as the new owners of the house. We invited him to speak to us or appear before us if he were capable of performing such a feat, and waited patiently for a reply or a manifestation. Nothing. We then politely asked several times if he could at least give us a sign in the form of a loud sound to let us know he was there. Within a few moments, we felt a strange chill around us and heard one very loud knock coming from the door at the end of the corridor. We had no doubt that it was the spirit of Dr. Crockett obliging us with the sign we requested.

My husband and I experienced a great deal of paranormal activity during our first year in the house, including numerous encounters with a phantom feline that would make his presence known by brushing itself against our legs. This would usually occur when we'd be eating a meal in the dining room or sitting at the desk and working on the computer. Each time we would feel it brushing against us, we would instinctively look down to see what was causing the sensation but nothing would ever be there. At least nothing that was visible to our eyes. In time the spirit would manifest itself to Brian and this would usually happen in the master bedroom where it would scurry across the floor and jump up onto the windowsill before vanishing into thin air. As of this writing, Brian has seen the cat close to a dozen times.

I've never seen the ghost cat myself but one afternoon I did witness a dark silhouette of a heavyset woman in a long dress standing silent and motionless on the servants' stairs at the back of the mansion. It gave me quite a bit of a start as I wasn't expecting to see anyone or anything standing there as I walked past. But no sooner had I focused my eyes upon the apparition, it was gone. It took a few minutes for me to regain my composure but I must admit I was feeling more excited than fearful. The experience also left me wondering if I had perhaps encountered the first lady of the house, Elizabeth Farnam, or maybe her servant, Jennie Bergen.

With all the activity that we were experiencing here Brian and I thought a séance might be a good idea. We chose the 17th of November as the date on which to hold it because it was the anniversary date of Stephen H. Farnam's death and it seemed appropriate. Our séance turned out to be a small one with only three people attending—Brian, myself and a friend. However, our sitting on that cold and windy November night proved to be quite an intense experience!

Seated at a round antique tiger-oak table with our hands joined to form a circle, we began the séance at ten-o'clock. I called out to the spirits of all the persons who had died in the house, inviting them to communicate with us and to give us a sign that they were here. Not long after we began hearing creaking sounds coming from different parts of the house and could feel the temperature in the room dropping. Brian sensed there were a number of spirits, perhaps as many as a half dozen, now with us in the room. At that point we began taking turns asking various questions such as what were their names, did they approve of the work we had done on the house, why were they not at peace and so forth.

Brian opened himself up to the spirits and entered a trance-like state in which he was able to pass along messages from the other side that he "heard" intuitively. But eventually he began to feel overwhelmed by the spirits who were all clamoring to speak to him at the same time and then the strange and disturbing sensation of something attempting to take control of his mind and body. Reacting with anger, he pounded his fist down on the top of the table and yelled, "Get out!"

At that precise moment we all heard a strange ear-piercing sound blaring throughout the house. It sounded almost like an air-horn and lasted for about three or four seconds. We were all quite startled and took to our feet looking around in a vain attempt to discover what it was that had caused the sound. Just then I happened to glance over to Dr. H.'s mirror out in the hall and spotted the reflection of a dark shadow darting up the stairs to the second floor. We all went upstairs to investigate it but there was nothing to be found.

I had attended quite a few séances prior to this one but never ever experienced anything quite like that before. It's something I don't think I'll ever forget for as long as I live! My only regret is that we didn't have a video camera, or at least a voice recorder, taping during and after the séance.

In 2011, after a lot of planning and hard work, the doors to the Collinwood Inn Bed and Breakfast officially opened attracting *Dark Shadows* fans of all ages and from all parts of the world. And, not surprisingly, some of our guests have reported strange unexplained phenomena while staying here, ranging from ghost cats in their rooms to lights turning on and off by themselves. Other people have witnessed apparitions, shadow figures, ghostly voices and strange sounds and sensations. Many who have experienced these things are convinced, as are we, that the spirits of those who have died in the Farnam Mansion have never left the house.

In April of 2011, we called in the New York Shadow Chasers to conduct a paranormal investigation at the Collinwood Inn and document any ghostly activity they might encounter in the house. During the seven-hour-long investigation, a lamp in the parlor switched on by itself and unexplained footsteps were heard coming from an empty bedroom directly above. A shadow figure was also witnessed by the investigators, equipment registered fluctuating and abnormally high readings, numerous spirits communicated verbally through a PX box (a device that converts environmental energy around the box into an electronic voice) and other paranormal phenomena was witnessed and recorded. The evidence, which includes a walk-through tour of the mansion, was posted on *YouTube* for all to see.

In early July 2011, one of Dr. H's daughters paid us a surprise visit and asked if we would be willing to give her and her family a tour of the house. She was in town for the Independence

Day weekend and said she would like to show her son the house in which she and her siblings had grown up. (It was also the house where both of her parents had died). We consented and the next day she arrived with her husband, her son and his wife, her sister and her brother and his three children. Brian showed them around and as soon as they entered the parlor a strange thing happened, which was witnessed by everyone. The crystal chandelier in the main hall went off by itself and moments later a table lamp in the parlor mysteriously came on. After that, the conversation turned to ghosts and the three siblings began recalling stories of hearing unexplained footsteps and other strange noises in the house that frightened them when they were children.

Some people might explain this away by blaming faulty wiring. However, the chandelier had never turned off by itself prior to that afternoon and so far has not done it since. We've also had the wiring checked by a licensed home inspector before buying the house and by a professional electrician who has done electrical work for us in the house more than once and both told us that the wiring is in excellent condition. We believe the incident was paranormal in nature and was actually Dr. H's and his wife's way of saying hello to their children and grandchildren and letting them know that they're still here.

However, that was not the only strange thing to happen at the Collinwood Inn involving an electric light fixture. One evening while I was sitting at the computer doing some research on the history of the mansion and the area, I stumbled upon a number of old newspaper articles concerning the original owner, Stephen H. Farnam. One article was about how his axe factory in Little Falls, New York, was destroyed by a flood in 1864. Another article told of how he lost his hardware business in Oneida to a devastating fire in 1890, sustaining a $20,000 loss but only being insured up to $14,000. Other ones revealed a mortgage foreclosure in 1894, a robbery at the mansion in 1864 and even how the sheriff closed his son's hardware store on September 27, 1893 on $12,000 judgments in favor of the National State Bank and Stephen H. Farnam.

As I was reading the articles to Brian a strange feeling suddenly came over him and he looked at me and said, "I don't think Stephen is very happy with you prying into his private life like this." I replied by chuckling, which apparently was not at all appreciated, because a moment later there was an exploding sound and the glass part of one of the light bulbs in the kitchen's hanging light fixture detached from the metal part that screws into the socket and flew like a rocket across the room with its elements glowing red and smoke trailing from it. As I picked up the bulb from the floor I felt compelled to apologize to Mr. Farnam for my insolence and assured him that I meant no disrespect.

On August 13, 2011 we hosted our first "Night of Shadows" event. The public (as well as the media) was invited to join us and four members of the New York Shadow Chasers for a paranormal investigation and Victorian-style séance at the bed and breakfast. A total of thirteen people attended, two of which reserved our popular Barnabas Room for the night.

The evening started off with a meet and greet, followed by a "Ghost Hunting 101" in which the New York Shadow Chasers discussed and demonstrated the equipment they utilize during their investigations. Afterwards, the investigation was officially underway and the investigators and guests made their way through the house armed with cameras, electromagnetic field meters, voice recorders and other gadgets in the hope of finding evidence of paranormal activity.

During the course of the investigation a

number of EVPs (electronic voice phenomenon) were recorded in the attic, digital cameras captured orbs and banging noises were heard at various locations on the second floor. During the séance the loud sound of furniture being dragged across the room could be heard coming from one of the guest rooms. The room was immediately investigated but there was no one in it, none of the furniture had been moved out of place and nothing looked to be disturbed.

Our resident ghost cat, which had so often made its presence known to Brian and me by brushing against our legs, made a brief appearance to Shadow Chaser founder Phillip Creighton that evening, stirring up a bit of a commotion. After Phillip opened the attic door and began climbing the steps leading to the attic he was met by the white cat, which he said came running down the steps towards him. He was so startled that he nearly lost his balance and fell backwards. The cat vanished and luckily nobody was injured.

The following morning during breakfast Brian and I were informed by our guests, who had spent the night in the Barnabas Room, that one of them was awakened around 5:00 a.m. by the sound of doors creaking and a man's voice coming from her private bathroom. She also told us that she heard a man's voice whisper in her ear, "It's over there," and was so unnerved by the experience that she was unable to return to sleep and too frightened to get out of bed to turn on her camcorder.

Like many of our other guests, she arrived at the Collinwood Inn a skeptic, and checked out with little or no doubt in her mind that within the red brick walls of the old Farnam Mansion dwell the shadows of the unexplained.

For more information about the Collinwood Inn Bed and Breakfast please visit their website at http://collinwoodinn.webs.com.

ROME

ERIE CANAL VILLAGE

Disembodied voices, uncanny apparitions and strange smells are commonplace in the Erie Canal Village. The outdoor living history museum is recreated on the site where construction began on the Erie Canal in 1817. The settlement is home to three museums—the Erie Canal Museum, the Harden Museum which exhibits a collection of horse drawn vehicles and the New York State Museum of Cheese which once housed the Merry and Weeks cheese factory in nearby Verona.

In addition to the museums, other 19th century structures include Bennett's Tavern, Blacksmith Shop, Railroad Station, Ice House, Wood Creek School, Maynard Methodist Church, Shull Victorian House, Settler's House, Crosby House and the Canal Store. Any lingering spirits certainly have their choice of real estate to haunt but it seems that there are a few preferred properties...

Melody Meluski's dog follows her everywhere. One day as the Museum Director stood on the tavern's porch she heard her pooch give a yelp then come running through the screen door from inside. No body was in the tavern at the time yet the dog refuses to go back inside the building. Also as a worker performed his maintenance duties on the tavern's second floor, he distinctly heard a disembodied male voice order him to leave. The worker was the only person on site and when he looked around to see who may have spoken he found no one.

Full-bodied apparitions manifest in the Harden carriage museum, women's screams emanate from the Victorian homes set on the property, strange noises originate from the train depot and musket fire is discerned coming from the former Fort Bull.

Fort Bull was built on the upper landing of Wood Creek to protect the Oneida Carry during the French and Indian War. A bloody massacre transpired at the fort and created an intense emotional imprint of embedded energy. Ken Ernenwein, a ghost hunter from Verona Paranormal Investigations, smelled cigar smoke while investigating the Fort Bull location. Eric Meier of New York Shadow Chasers detected the sound of cannon fire and smelled a sulfurous burn in the air.

When New York State Paranormal Research conducted a month-long investigation they discovered eerie occupants inhabiting several sites as well. Investigators Cano Davy and Marcus Zwierecki write:

> *"Paranormal claims range from voices to apparitions to poltergeist activity. We were amazed by the amount of activity encountered. During the investigation at Bennett's Tavern we set up our Digital Video Recorder (DVR) system*

with four infrared cameras along with digital recorders and motion sensors. We left the building unattended after set-up was complete. We then headed to the Harden Museum. Unbeknown to us, while down in the museum, we captured EVPs and someone or something set off the motion sensor. One EVP sounds like a grumpy man saying, 'Why are they here?' Cameras covered all building entrances so we know there was nobody in the location at this time. While investigating the Harden Museum, Marcus and Cano set up an infrared handheld camera on the first floor and proceeded to investigate the top floor. We managed to capture video footage of a strange light orb moving from left to right, but what really makes this video strange is the snapping sound heard as the orb begins to move. When EVP or video activity is captured, we often notice precursors to the activity.

Over four hundred photos were taken but the only photograph that appears to reveal an anomaly is a strange photo we captured at Fort Bull. Fort Bull is one of three forts built in the Erie Canal region during the French and Indian War; the fort was destroyed centuries ago along with scores of soldiers defending the land."

FORT STANWIX

Fort Stanwix is situated on an original Oneida carrying place—the Iroquois Nation's portage used to bridge the Mohawk River and Wood Creek. Built in 1758, the stronghold safeguarded the Mohawk Valley's major thoroughfare during the French and Indian War.

During the Revolutionary War, British military forces were resisted as they attempted to capture the fort. American militiamen and Oneida allies tried to aid Fort Stanwix but they were ambushed at Oriskany, one of the revolt's bloodiest clashes.

A colorful chapter concerning our nation's flag occurred when Fort Stanwix defenders decided to fashion a standard to fly over the fort. For the blue they used a cloak captured from a British officer, regular army shirts served as the white stripes and stars and the red material came from a woman's flannel petticoat.

Much like the ghostly goings-on at several other ancient New York forts, spectral soldiers in period dress materialize in various places throughout the garrison. At sunrise, musical strains from phantom fifes and drums occasionally filter from the fortress and echo in the valley.

Other spine-chilling happenings include the disembodied sound of a woman weeping. Some tourists spotted a male apparition with only one leg sitting in the barracks. Most astoundingly, an unknown spirit carries on his chores from the great beyond evidenced by neatly swept floors and a steady supply of newly chopped firewood— the kind of ambitious ghost we all want haunting our homes!

The Northern Paranormal Society conducted several EVP sessions and captured male voices in the hospital building and on the parade grounds. The team also captured the oft reported phantom flute or fife music.

ORISKANY BATTLEFIELD

On August 6, 1777, the British commanded Colonel Barry St. Leger to embark on the Mohawk Valley and destroy all settlements. The colonel decided to attack Fort Stanwix before proceeding down river.

Brigadier General Nicholas Herkimer organized 800 militiamen, supported by 60 Oneida warriors, against St. Leger's troops. As Herkimer advanced, the opposition set a trap in a swampy ravine west of Oriskany Creek.

As unsuspecting American troops crossed the bog and marched up the ravine the British attacked. Mortal combat ensued, and even though they teetered on victory, the enemy retreated. The ambush left General Herkimer mortally wounded—over half his troops and Oneida allies were dead, injured or captured.

The Battle of Oriskany is described as one of the bloodiest engagements of the American Revolution. Considered a significant turning point in the struggle for independence, a monument dedicated on the site memorializes those who sacrificed to secure freedom. Oriskany Battlefield is a designated New York State historic site since 1927 and a National Historic Landmark since 1963. Today, visitors to the battlefield can walk the site, read interpretive signs, visit a historic encampment during special events and perhaps experience something supernatural...

Battlefields are notoriously haunted places. Philip Freneau, the Poet of the American Revolution aptly wrote:

"Where Death in ten-fold vengeance
holds his reign,
And injured ghosts, yet unavenged
complain."

At Oriskany Battlefield the awful struggle appears to persist…Some visitors who walk the ravine sense a palpable presence of unseen militia. Neighbors often hear the cries and screams of spectral soldiers. Motorists sometimes observe fiery gunfire sparks and orbs floating in the woods—all chilling anomalies and reminders revealing the enduring effects of war.

New York State Paranormal Research reports:

"We were conducting an investigation in the field when Cano turned on the recorder and stated the time, date, and location. After reviewing the recorders we listened to two recorded voices. One is where a gentleman with an English accent can be heard saying, 'Recording' as if mimicking Cano's voice. In the second recording, a voice is heard when we are leaving which sounds like 'stumble.' Throughout the night we randomly encountered a foul stench. We set out to find the cause of the odor but to no avail.

We found the spot next to the stream where we believed the ambush occurred and began an ITC Box session. We began to snap photos. In one photo we captured a man's face in the lower left hand corner. This battlefield possesses the 'feel' of history and mystery."

ROME CAPITOL THEATRE

One of the most fashionable Mohawk Valley haunts is the Capitol Theatre at 220 West Dominick Street. The theater opened on December 10, 1928 as part of the Kallet Brothers' chain of movie houses presenting first run films. For nearly 50 years, the Capitol Theatre was Rome's premiere movie house with seating for 2,500, a Möller theater organ in the orchestra pit and two projectors designed for "talking pictures."

Over the years, Bing Crosby and other entertainers performed on the Capitol stage. The Dorsey Brothers Orchestra performed in 1954 and two years later Bill Haley & the Comets played to the crowd who danced in the aisles.

Due to high overhead costs, the Capitol closed in 1974. The final film shown was *The Exorcist* (!). Interestingly, the Cinema National movie theatre chain leased the old theater until 1989, not for exhibition, but simply to avert competition with the chain's multiplex.

Over the next eleven years the Capitol occasionally accommodated live events. By 1985 the performing arts center became a reality thanks to a group of dedicated individuals. Rome's citizens eagerly anticipated the theater's re-emergence as the Capitol Civic Center. Opening night featured a screening of *Lilac Time*, the film originally screened on opening night at the Capitol in 1928.

Today the Capitol hosts over 100 performances every year—from the continuing live theatrical performances of SummerStage to world famous big bands such as Glenn Miller, Artie Shaw and Tommy Dorsey, dance programs and classic silent and talking films.

Theaters are notoriously haunted places

and the Capitol is no exception. Spooky reports first emerged more than thirty years ago with accounts of a ghostly figure in the balcony. The male shadow figure that is sometimes observed is presumed to be a former projectionist or a phantom performer as the mysterious form haunts both the balcony and stage. A ghostly cat also stalks about the theater. Phantom organ music resounds (even when the organ was inoperable until its repair in 2003). Whispered conversations, doors opening mysteriously and even spectral sounds of dramatic performances are experienced by late night theatergoers and playhouse personnel.

When the Ghost Seekers of Central New York investigated the historic theater doors opened and slammed shut as the paranormal team performed their research. They experienced an extreme fluctuation in temperature on the stage and near the balcony.

During Davy/Zwierecki and their NYSPR investigative team's visit, their survey elicited the following results:

"This investigation was a short one for us as we only had a four hour play time including set up and break down so we had to get up and get

*going quickly. On this investigation we split up
into two teams. Cano and John P. headed to the
basement to begin their investigation and Marcus
and Justin R. headed to the balcony. Apparitions
and shadow people are seen throughout the
building; disembodied voices and footsteps are
heard inside as well. While in the basement
Cano headed upstairs to get fresh batteries.
While up there, John asked the spirits to make
a noise for him—in response, mumbling can be
heard on the audiotape but what is being said is
unclear. After an hour the two teams switched
locations. While on the second floor balcony,
Cano snapped photos aimed at the stage area.
After reviewing the footage he captured a shadow
person (photo and EVPs on NYSPR website:
www.newyorkstateparanormalresearch.com).
John and Cano then conducted an EVP session.
During this period a commotion ensued from
an unoccupied room only feet away. There was
a recorder in the room and the ruckus can be
heard very clearly. Also in the cellar…when we
first arrived the temperature was a steady 67
degrees throughout the entire basement. Suddenly
the temperature dropped to 55 degrees and
maintained that temperature for a minute or so
and then began to rise to 67 degrees once again."*

SAUQUOIT

ORCHARD HALL

Julia is the specter who resides at 2955 Oneida Street in Sauquoit. Allegedly, the victim of an errant bullet, the woman's luminescent apparition manifested to owner Sharon Puleo two years after she and her husband purchased the 19th century building. Sharon could hardly believe her eyes as she watched the white figure float down the stairway, enter the kitchen, come back out and glide back up the stairs.

The couple heard rumors about ghosts and haunting activity at the place but buried this thought as they breathed new life into the historic restaurant and bowling hall.

Built around 1843 upon land granted to a soldier by George Washington during the Revolutionary War, Orchard Hall came into existence as a stately home and later served as a

safe house on the Underground Railroad. Down
in the cellar covert passageways sheltered slaves
passing through Oneida, a secret escape route.
Some say Julia formerly held title to the property
and actively assisted the freedom seekers.

One psychic detected a black man's presence
wearing old-fashioned clothes in the basement.
Workers are reluctant to go down there because
they get the feeling someone is watching them.

Julia's ghost primarily dwells in one of the nine upstairs bedrooms where her apparition was once observed rocking in a rocking chair. Two musicians stayed overnight in that spirited room and rushed out at dawn after a sleepless night. During their stay a terrifying racket ensued. Doors slammed, terrible crashing noises reverberated and frightening footsteps kept the guests up all night. Sharon forgot to inform them about Julia!

Passersby often claim to see a light in the upstairs bedroom and a female silhouette standing at the window. Some contend that most likely Julia gave up the ghost in that room, so to speak.

Psychic mediums describe Julia as a woman in her thirties and dressed in a Victorian-era gown. When a diner expressed an appreciation for the portrayal of an authentically garbed 19th century woman traipsing through the dining room, co-owner Gary Puleo felt puzzled. The proprietors didn't hire any re-enactor but felt certain they knew who strolled through restaurant.

After hours, while contractors installed a new heating system, they heard someone upstairs banging about the kitchen. They assumed Gary made the noise and fully expected the owner to come down and greet them. He never did. The next day when the workmen questioned

Gary—neither he, nor any other living soul occupied the building the night before.

Other curious after-hour oddities are staffers sometimes hear phantom bowlers and detect the pungent odor of cigar smoke or the sweet scent of perfume. Cold spots are commonly reported in the ladies' room and one female patron got chills when she heard a woman cough—particularly because the customer knew she was alone in the restroom.

Cano Davy of NYSPR writes:

"The owners are very much aware and accepting of the spirits who linger throughout this historic location. On one occasion the owner, Sharon, witnessed Julia, the resident ghost descending from the second floor landing.

During our investigation in the basement (which is believed to once be a safe haven for runaway slaves) we conducted a flashlight experiment; we would ask yes/ no questions to which the flashlight would turn on for yes or off for no. Marcus states just for verification could you please turn the middle flashlight on three times. Suddenly right on cue the middle flashlight turned off and on three times. While on the second floor Marcus asked if they could respond to questions being asked; a reply of 'Yes' was captured.

We left a recorder running on the first floor for the investigation's duration. We managed to capture a female voice saying 'Get out!' Then, in the infamous room on the second floor where the overnight guests were run out, we left a recorder sitting on the fireplace mantel where we captured a creepy EVP. Unfortunately, we cannot make out what is being said but it sounds like a child whispering loudly. A photo revealed an image also captured in this room; we sent this picture to a photo expert who states she cannot technically explain the appearance of the figure.

We did not feel threatened at all but did not feel as if we were alone either."

ST. JOHNSVILLE

BEARDSLEE CASTLE

Augustus Beardslee built the spooky-looking castle on Route 5, between Little Falls and St. Johnsville, in 1860 to replicate an Irish fortress. His son, Captain Guy Beardslee was born in the mansion and ultimately graduated from West Point. Beardslee constructed a dam and power plant to furnish electricity, not only for his own farms, but also for the Village of St. Johnsville. Streetlights illuminated the village for the first time on March 17, 1898.

According to historical records, a fortified homestead stood on the wilderness site in 1750. Legend says a tunnel led from the main house into a hill where munitions were stored. During a raid on the fortress, Native Americans accidentally set off the gunpowder with their torches. The natives were annihilated. The burrow's entrance is in the basement (known as "ghost central") and even though the shaft is sealed by boulders ghostly activity down here is attributed to restless Indian spirits. Since the site also served as a stop on the Underground Railroad, slaves most likely hid in the passageway. Do their spirits linger here or is it Dominie Jake? More on him later...

All sorts of unexplained phenomena occur at the creepy castle and are ascribed to a hefty phantom population. Sadly, one of Beardslee's sons drowned nearby. The boy's spirit is often heard playing in the stone structure. Captain Beardslee's ghost roams the grounds at night. He holds a lantern aloft to illumine his path. Several auto accidents in the area are attributed to Beardslee's wandering spirit and his confounding light which catches driver's off guard, to put it mildly.

"Pop" Anton M. Christensen purchased the property from Mrs. Beardslee and opened the mansion as a restaurant in 1941. He lost his wife, became despondent and ultimately committed suicide by hanging. His frightening specter shows up dangling from a noose in the dark recess upstairs where he took his life.

After hours, staffers hear indiscernible voices and resounding footsteps, light orbs float through rooms, lights are found glowing when turned off the night before, doors locked at closing are unlocked in the morning, and an ungodly shriek, called the "Big Scream," resonates throughout the structure, its source unknown.

In *Ghostly American Places* author Arthur Myers recounts an experience by an employee. The staffer experienced a deathly cold chill then observed a disembodied hand, which appeared like an x-ray image; she could easily discern the bones. Soon after, a co-worker observed a man dressed in a top hat and black suit standing in the same archway where the hand appeared; the Abe Lincoln-like image quickly dissipated.

A party guest captured a similar dark apparition on film. This entity frequently appears and those in the know identify him as Dominie Jake. The deacon allegedly molested children, says Myers who researched the castle's chronicles. The disgraced clergyman purportedly hanged himself in the underground passageway.

An odd cast of ghostly characters calls the castle home. There's the specter who sits in a wingback chair by the fireplace even though, in reality, there is no seating arranged there. A flaxen-haired wraith in a full-length dress frequents the ladies room. One worker observed a woman in a dressing gown carrying a bed tray up an invisible flight of stairs (before the remodel, a staircase existed there).

Once a diner peered into an upstairs banquet room and observed a foursome enjoying a candlelight dinner. Together with a server the pair investigated the room and found the area empty.

"Abigail" is yet another entity who supposedly served at the manor and choked to death. Her spirit speaks to the wait staff whispering their names (and giving them the heebie-jeebies!).

Not surprisingly, Beardslee Castle attracts ghost hunters who have succeeded in recording chilling voices. In 1983, Norm Gauthier, an investigator from the New Hampshire Institute for Paranormal Research, was called in to get to the root of the castle's eerie claims. Gauthier captured chilling, whispered voices and concluded Beardslee Manor was definitely haunted by at least two spirits.

In 1999, Beardslee Castle was featured on a segment of *Haunted History* on the History Channel. In 2008, TAPS (The Atlantic Paranormal Society) highlighted Beardslee Castle as a finalist on their *Ghost Hunters* "Great American Ghost Hunt" Halloween Special. Beardslee Castle was the runner-up.

FORT KLOCK

Johannes Klock constructed a stone house on the Mohawk River in 1750. Settlers sought refuge in the stronghold during the French and Indian and Revolutionary Wars. The National Historic Landmark on Route 5 in St. Johnsville exemplifies a mid-18th century fur trading post and fortified house structure. The fort is fully restored and operates as a museum.

During the War for Independence imprisoned and wounded British soldiers and their Indian allies were held captive in Fort

Klock's cellar until they could be transferred to another location. The men were cruelly secured to the wall by thick, heavy chains—the relics remain intact to this day. So do the gruesome bloodstains forever defacing the stone floor—another gory remnant.

According to historical records, one poor Brit sustained a serious gunshot wound. Shackled to the cold stone wall he perished from his injuries during a frigid winter night. Unable to bury his body in the frozen earth, his remains were cremated in the field, along with several other comrades who also fell in battle.

Speculatively, because no grave or stone marker exists to commemorate his death, the soldier's spirit is trapped in the vault where he died. Late at night, his moans emanate from the deathly cold cellar.

UTICA

FIRST PRESBYTERIAN CHURCH

Robert MacKinnon, a well-educated and much admired Scottish immigrant, made his fortune in the milling industry in Cohoes and Little Falls. In 1898, he moved his family north for greater cultural opportunities and erected the greatest home ever built in Utica. C. Edward Vosbury designed the manse at 1605 Genesee Street. Vosbury also designed the Alonzo Roberson Mansion in Binghamton. (Oddly, the Roberson Mansion is also haunted! See the author's *Ghosts of Central New York*).

In June 1910, MacKinnon hosted a grand wedding for his daughter. Thousands of flowers enthralled the 700 guests who attended the gala. Ironically, by year's end the businessman suffered a reversal of fortune and lost everything.

MacKinnon endured further trials. Shortly after her wedding the daughter and her husband, who owned one-third of Jamaica, moved to the island where she died shortly thereafter. Another daughter mysteriously disappeared in 1916. A third daughter died in a New York City hospital charity ward and MacKinnon's reclusive son lived out his days in a veteran's hospital.

The MacKinnon House languished for years and the First Presbyterian Church eventually acquired the property at 1605 Genesee Street. Possibly the family's lonely spirits remain to recapture happier days.

Mohawk Valley Ghost Hunters checked out the alleged paranormal activity at the church. Equipped with infrared cameras and other high-tech equipment, the group detected an "active presence" and filmed darting light globules in the church sanctuary.

In addition, the church secretary and the church custodian, George Abel, got goose bumps when they observed a phantom female, wearing an ivory gown, glide down the grand staircase.

Inexplicably, visitors to the third floor ballroom often proclaim they feel a backwards shove. This leads to another perplexing incident that occurred while Abel tended to his duties. Losing his footing on a ladder he began a plummet that meant certain injury. Suddenly, unseen hands caught him and averted his fall. This spirit was far from pushy—Abel feels the rescue was divine intercession.

New York State Paranormal Researcher Cano Davy writes:

"The Presbyterian Church is one of the more active locations we investigated in the Mohawk Valley. During our first two investigations we captured minimal evidence but on our third and fourth investigations we had personal experiences and captured some great evidence. Marcus investigated the first floor and Cano the third floor. While conducting a session Marcus passed by a specific spot in the church where he became overwhelmed by dizziness. Unbeknown to Cano, an hour or so later while on the first floor, he also walked by the same location in the church and became very lightheaded to the point where he dropped to one knee to regain his balance. Later, as we packed our equipment, Marcus mentioned his dizziness. Before he could say any more Cano asked Marcus to show him the area where this reaction occurred. Lo' and behold it was the exact same spot where Cano's encounter occurred. We tried to get a reading from the Trifield®Meter, knowing a high EMF reading may be the cause

for both of us to experience the same feeling at the same location. However, this time we did not capture a high EMF reading.

On our last investigation we did manage to capture a few audio anomalies. We were both on the third floor conducting an EVP session, taking photos, documenting a baseline EMF and temperature reading. During this time the telephone rang only once. While reviewing our audio on a later date, after the phone rings a woman can be heard saying the name 'Cano.' A previous incident in the Presbyterian Church occurred when phones would ring and the call would be coming from a room in the securely locked and vacant building. Again on the third floor Marcus and Cano are talking about our battery situation. Every time we replace batteries they would completely drain in seconds. As we are discussing this a voice can be heard whispering the name 'Cano' again. We believe this spirit presence is most likely the reason we experienced sapped batteries.

In addition, on our last investigation we captured a disembodied voice, although what is being said is unclear. Occurrences experienced throughout this location range from K2 hits to cold spots to disembodied voices."

ONEIDA COUNTY
HISTORICAL SOCIETY

In 1876, the Oneida County Historical Society was founded at 1608 Genesee Street. The historical society collects artifacts, information and memorabilia to preserve Oneida County's heritage.

George Abel is a volunteer at both the Oneida County Historical Society and the First Presbyterian Church. Abel performs custodial work at the buildings to maintain their condition. As Abel worked late one particular evening at the historical society, he began his routine to close down the building for the night. Approaching the front door to lock up, he spotted a man wearing a dark suit walk about ten feet ahead of him. The stranger headed for the stairs to the balcony. Abel announced to the man that the historical society was closing. By the time Abel reached the front door he lost sight of the man. The custodian thought the visitor wandered upstairs so Abel went to find him. He searched the upper floor and eventually the entire building but found no one. The man would have to pass by Abel to get back down the steps!

Another time when teenagers showed up, it soon became apparent the kids bore no interest in history. Their goal was to fool around. Abel shadowed them but the boys ran upstairs. They quickly arrived downstairs looking like they had seen a ghost. "Who's the old lady in the black dress?" they asked in passing. Abel sensed their fright and the boys left on their own—they couldn't get out fast enough!

At one time the building served as a hospice for tuberculosis patients and the second floor was referred to as the "sick room." Ghost Seekers of Central New York recorded sighs of distress twice in the sick room. A whistle caught on a digital recorder appears to be in response to a ghost hunter's request to the spirits to whistle or sing. They recorded a ghostly image on film form, disappear then form again!

New York State Paranormal Research investigators write:

"We heard about the activity going on at the Oneida County Historic Society from a friend. We interviewed witnesses who claimed children witnessed a woman in a white dress walking up the stairs and when they turned around to tell somebody, she was no longer there. The second claim alleges a man was seen walking in the building at the close of business by caretaker George Abel. Mr. Abel proceeded to go and tell the 'man' that the Historic Society was closed for the night and no one was to be found in the building.

Local news station WUTR shadowed us throughout the night on our investigation and did a piece for a show called 'Hello Central New York.' During the night the atmosphere felt strange; it was as if an electrical charge flowed through the building. Noises and footsteps could be heard coming from what is called the 'sick room' on the second floor—a hospice area where people succumbed to tuberculosis. At certain times it sounded as if boxes were being moved around. We captured a male voice yelling, 'Out.' Everyone agreed they felt as if they were not alone."

RUTGER PARK MANSIONS

Rutger-Steuben Park Historic District is a national historic neighborhood that includes a private section known as Rutger Park. Five architecturally significant dwellings are clustered in the center of Rutger Park. The elegant mansions reflect Utica's prosperity between 1830 and 1890. The opening of the Erie and Chenango Canals, the establishment of the textile industry along Oriskany and Sauquoit Creeks and the building of railroads brought major economic growth to the Mohawk Valley, particularly the City of Utica. Two of the five houses are owned by the Landmarks Society of Greater Utica and they are notoriously haunted.

ONE RUTGER PARK

In 1854, Alexander Jackson Davis, one of the most influential and innovative figures in American architecture, designed the residence at One Rutger Park for banker John Munn. During the Civil War,

Samuel Remington resided there when Remington
Arms ran a factory in Utica. (Odd that the
Winchester Mystery House in San Jose, California,
also home to a gun magnate, is notoriously
haunted!) The architectural plans for the Italian
Villa style dwelling are in the permanent collection
at the Metropolitan Museum of Art.

Walter Jerome Green Jr. served as President of Utica Investment Company and the Utica City National Bank and Director of First National Bank and Trust Company. He resided at One Rutger Park from age four (1880) until his death in 1951. The distinctive home possessed an elevator and a giant turntable in the garage since back in the day automobiles lacked a reverse gear.

These days stories of restless spirits revolve about the beautiful mansion. The most mysterious phenomenon experienced at the historic house is the sighting of a disembodied spirit moving about the foyer. K2 meters light up like Luna Park indicating an ephemeral presence.

THREE RUTGER PARK

 The Green's neighbor at Rutger Park was Roscoe Conkling, a staunch Lincoln supporter and a 1870s United States Senator from New York State and one of the nation's most powerful Republicans during President

Ulysses S. Grant's administration. Called "the power behind the throne," Conkling also befriended and mentored the 21st President of the United States, Chester Arthur (1881–1885).

Three Rutger Park hosted important parties attended by Generals U. S. Grant, Sherman and Hooker of the Civil War; all went on to lucrative careers in the railroad industry and government service after the war.

When Ghost Seekers of Central New York investigated the property a spirit shoved a team member into a closet and tugged on their pants. The investigators watched in awe as ectoplasm shrouded the stairway then transformed into a male apparition. Could this awesome ghost be the powerful senator?

New York State Paranormal Research findings:

"These particular buildings have been on our radar for quite some time. We began the night by setting up four infrared cameras in Building #3 along with four digital audio recorders. Investigators that night were Cano, Marcus, John and Justin. We also invited two other investigators from two other groups Ken Ernenwein, founder of Verona Paranormal Investigations, and NYSPR associate Amber Poole. After setting up equipment in #3 we moved on to Building #1. We set up a total of four infrared cameras and four digital recorders in this location also. We then split up into two teams. Throughout the night in Building #1 we managed to capture a fair share of EVP. The first was in the basement of #1...Marcus asks, 'Do you need help?' to which a female says, 'Help me.' We were using the ITC box, which is becoming a very valuable piece of equipment. Moments later we say that we are getting ready to leave, and can they say 'Good bye' to which we receive a reply of

'Goodbye.' *The voice sounds like the first female voice. We managed to capture EVP throughout both buildings that night. We also managed to capture a strange light anomaly in Building #3. This 'thing' comes into frame and leaves as fast as anything. When this video is slowed down the light is moving very 'intelligently.' It darts from one room into the next room then peeks out of the door only to keep playing a peek- a- boo type game. The light maintains a very bright illumination the entire time except before it darts off—then it changes to a smoky gray color. The team has watched videos for several years now and our recordings have never captured anything like this...very strange. We are looking forward to going back for a new investigation, this location has much more going on then we first thought... We captured a total of 12 EVPs that night."*

MOHAWK VALLEY CRYSTALS

According to the book, *Mohawk: Discovering the Valley of the Crystals*, author M. Paul Keesler regards the Mohawks as the "people of the place of the crystals." Kessler asserts that double-faceted quartz crystals are unique to the Mohawk Valley. Also known as Herkimer Diamonds, Mohawk Valley crystals are major attractions in the region.

Quartz crystal can transmit and receive, amplify, focus, project and store energies thereby enhancing supernatural communication. The naturally formed doubly terminated crystals found in the Mohawk Valley are considered more powerful than crystals carved or cut into a double terminated form.

Quartz is believed to strengthen the link between heaven and earth enabling the user to see into other times and realities. The mineral's amplifying abilities can increase psychic awareness; its capability to channel energies empowers the detection of spirit forces and the recording of spirit images and voices.

Dedicated to the memory of
Diane L. Davy.

NEW YORK STATE PARANORMAL RESEARCH CO-FOUNDERS

To **CANO DAVY** paranormal investigation is more than a hobby or a pastime—it's a way of life. He began investigating the paranormal after a post-mortem encounter with his brother, Pete. When his brother Crandall passed away, Cano successfully helped to reunite the brothers in the afterlife via spirit intercession.

Cano appreciates his wife Alicia for her understanding and support of his life's journey. Especially for her patience with all the long nights he's away from home hunting ghosts!

Cano's 12-year-old son Jared is following in his father's footsteps. Jared maintains his own UFO web page. Cano and Jared share a passion for the unknown and Jared is first to review the evidence captured during NYSPR investigations. Whenever life speeds up and Cano gets down Jared's smile lifts him up to where he needs to be.

MARCUS ZWERICKI has always been interested in the beyond the here and now and paranormal research. A student of the paranormal since childhood, his knowledge is furthered by authors and researchers such as Hans Holzer. When skeptics ask if he's serious about ghost hunting Marcus suggests they look to belief systems, for in each and every one there are references to life after death.

First and foremost, Marcus is a family man. He and his wife Jessica are expecting their third daughter, Halia. Their other daughters are Autumn, who is 12, and Laila who passed away at 15 days old.

Marcus' enduring hope is to gain more and more knowledge, grow in stature as a paranormal researcher and to share his expertise by training others.

(Listen to EVP audio clips and view photographic/video evidence on the New York State Paranormal Research website: http://nysparanormalresearch.com).

Acknowledgements

This ghost story collection would not be possible without the spirits who haunt the locations; the individuals who witness the unexplainable anomalies and apparitions, hear the spooky noises, feel the chilling touches and smell the lingering odors; the ghost hunters who take temperature readings, capture orb-embedded photos, speak to the dead and record unnerving voices from beyond...*and* the following individuals:

The author especially thanks Cano Davy and Marcus Zwierecki. Cano and Marcus performed above and beyond their role as paranormal researchers. Besides providing investigative reports, they went the extra mile to obtain background material and photographs. Other NYSPR team members John Pauba, Justin D. Reynolds and Jared Christopher Sciortino assisted Cano and Marcus in the search for spirits.

Sincere appreciation to the following individuals for allowing access to the haunted properties and for offering information: Steve Best, First Presbyterian Church, Utica; Michael Bosak, Rutger Mansions; Sharon Dawn Coyle, Rolling Hills Asylum; Frank Daskiewich, Hulbert House; Michelle Forward, Library Manager, Morrisville Library; Gerri and Brian Gray, Collinwood Inn Bed and Breakfast; Jim Greiner, Herkimer County Historic Jail; Brian J. Howard, Executive Director, Oneida County Historic Society; Melody Milewski, Erie Canal Village; Sharon Puleo, Orchard Hall; David Taylor, Little Falls' Stone Mill at Canal Place; Jack Theakston, Capitol Theater; Eileen Warner, Indian Castle Church; and the Staff at Oriskany Battlefield.

Sincere gratitude to Gerri Rachel Gray of the Collinwood Inn for her story *The House of Many Shadows*; to Karen Bodmer Alfred of Things Remembered Photography and Joann Richmond, South Jersey Ghost Research for their consultation services; and most of all to my publishing partners, Deb Tremper, Graphic Designer and my friend, Maryann Way for guiding me through the intricate process of bringing forth this book.

Bibliography

Barefoot, Daniel W. *Spirits of '76: Ghost Stories of the American Revolution*. John F. Blair Publisher, 2009.

Borick, Anna. "The Haunting of Rolling Hills." *Ghost Magazine*, 2007.

Cudmore, Bob. "Mohawk Valley's Ghost Stories." *The Daily Gazette*, October 31, 2010.

Edwards, Phillip A. "Capitol Theatre's old Möller organ gets a dramatic new lift." Rome Grand Theatre Organ Society, http://www.theatreorgans.com/ny/rome.

Greene, Nelson (Editor). *History of the Mohawk Valley: Gateway to the West 1614–1925*. www.schenectadyhistory.org.

Keesler, M. Paul. *Mohawk: Discovering the Valley of the Crystals*. North Country Books, 2009.

Macken, Lynda Lee. *Ghosts of Central New York*. Black Cat Press, 2009.

Moore, Kathleen. "Ghosts are real deal on this tour." *The Daily Gazette*, October 21, 2005.

Myers, Arthur. *Ghostly American Places*. Gramercy Press, 1995.

Pitkin, David J. *New York State Ghosts,* Aurora Publications, 2006.

Reid, Max. *The Mohawk Valley, Its Legends and Its History*. The Knickerbocker Press, 1901.

Subar, Zach. "Knox Mansion ready for Halloween." *The Leader-Herald*, October 31, 2009.

Websites

Beardslee Castle: www.beardsleecastle.com

Central New York Ghost Hunters: www.gotghosts.org

Collinwood Inn: www.collinwoodinn.webs.com

Erie Canal Village: www.eriecanalvillage.net

Ghost Boxer: www.itcvoices.org

Ghost Seekers of Central New York: www.cnyghost.com

The Hulbert House: www.hulberthouse.com

Indian Castle Church: www.indiancastle.com

ISIS Paranormal Investigations: www.isisinvestigations.com

Klock Connections: www.klockconnections.com

Mohawk Valley Ghost Hunters: www.mvghntrs.tripod.com

M. Paul Keesler: www.mpaulkeesler.com

Nation Spiritualist Association: www.nsac.org

New York Shadow Chasers: www.nyshadowchasers.com

New York State Paranormal Research:
    www.nysparanormalresearch.com

The Northern Paranormal Society:
    www.thenorthernparanormalsociety.com

Oneida County Historical Society: www.oneidacountyhistory.org

Rolling Hills Asylum: www.rollinghillsasylum.vpweb.com

Rome Capitol Theatre: www.romecapitol.com

Rome Investigators of the Paranormal:
www.romeinvestigatorsoftheparanormal.com

Stone Mill of Little Falls: www.stonemilloflittlefalls.com

Thousand Islands Life: www.thousandislandslife.com

Three Rivers: www.threerivershms.com

Wikipedia: www.wikipedia.org

YouTube: www.youtube.com

Also by Lynda Lee Macken

Adirondack Ghosts

Adirondack Ghosts II

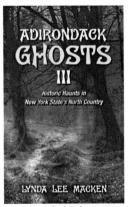

Adirondack Ghosts III

Empire Ghosts

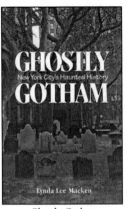

Ghostly Gotham

Ghosts of Central New York

Ghosts of the Garden State

*Ghosts of the
Garden State II*

*Ghosts of the
Garden State III*

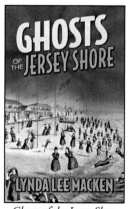

Ghosts of the Jersey Shore

Haunted Cape May

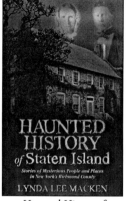

*Haunted History of
Staten Island*

Also by Lynda Lee Macken

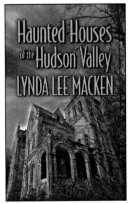

Haunted Houses
of the Hudson Valley

Haunted Lake George

Haunted Long Island

Haunted Long Island II

Haunted New Hope

Haunted Salem & Beyond

"When you see a ghost something very interesting happens. Your brain splits in two. One side of you is rejecting what you're seeing because it doesn't tally with our ordinary idea of reality and the other side is screaming, *but this is REAL!* And in that moment reality itself is collapsed and reconfigured in a way that changes you profoundly although at the time you're not aware of it."

—Conor McPherson, from the film *The Eclipse*

CPSIA information can be obtained at www.ICGtesting.com
Printed in the USA
BVOW020837101012

302587BV00004B/3/P